# GOLF ADDICTS
# ON PARADE

"OH, LOOK! IT'S GONE INTO MY BUNKER!"

# GOLF ADDICTS ON PARADE

Cartoons by

George Houghton

with an Introductory Foreword by

CYRIL TOLLEY

CHANCELLOR
PRESS

*First published in Great Britain 1959 by*
*Country Life Limited*

*This edition published 2003 by Chancellor Press,*
*an imprint of Bounty Books, a division of*
*Octopus Publishing Group Ltd,*
*2-4 Heron Quays, London E14 4JP*



*Printed and bound in Spain*

*ISBN 0 7537 0856 6*

CYRIL TOLLEY'S

# *Foreword*

IT was pleasant to be asked to take the honour on the first tee of this book of golf cartoons. I have respect and indeed affection for the artist and, realising that nothing I write can in any way detract from the merits and enjoyment of the drawings, I can relax (as a good golfer should) and take up my stance for this preliminary waggle.

First of all, let it be emphasised that the combination of brute force and something ignorance, pure skill, crowds of varying sizes, and a sprinkling of 'characters', have loaded the game of golf with more humour than can be found in practically any other walk of life. So George Houghton, a man who has steeped himself in this activity, has ample scope for his delightful form of illustration.

Analysing the ingredients : golf-crowd humour is of two varieties. A spectator supporting your opponent makes a wise-crack. This, you will decide, is in the height of bad taste. On the other hand, your own helping friends are nearly always pleasant and you can smile at anything they say.

The grotesque antics of players can be vastly amusing. A man I used to play with looked so much like a crab when he was putting that it took me a tremendous effort to prevent myself laughing out aloud. There was also the foreign Countess, whose posture on completion of numerous waggles resembled a praying mantis.

It is common knowledge that the author has spent a decade or so on the courses and links within reasonable reach of the metropolis. But as a matter of fact his particular brand of golfing nonsense started a long time ago. He went to the French Open Championship at St Cloud in 1932 to do cartoons for the *Daily Mail*, and had he not on this occasion libelled me so outrageously in caricature, I would recall that particular Championship with pleasure! On two previous occasions, both at La Boulie, I had won the tournament, and my visits to France were always a joy. In the early days, when Frenchmen were 'discovering' the game, apart from the great Arnaud Massy, they had few top-ranking players. But, as can be imagined, there was an abundance of first-class material for a golf humorist.

When in 1954 George Houghton was visiting the United States he suggested that, as I had resided for a few years between the wars in Uncle Sam's country, I might furnish names of devotees in and around New York. I complied most readily and with anticipated amusement sat back to await results. In a few months there was published a slim volume of his recorded impressions. He had energetically pulled the legs of all my friends and a totally new aspect of George's humour was unearthed and developed in a way easily discernible in this book.

Few people can seize upon incidents funny enough to stand the test of cold print. By wandering through the golfing scene with an ever-open notebook George Houghton seems to have succeeded. His cartoons are mostly based on odd snatches of conversation, often spoken with the utmost gravity. Seldom are his drawings really cruel. I can recall only one with a sting—'The trouble about Women Golfers is that they look like Women Golfers'. No doubt George has often suffered for that!

Thinking back over the years, one would have wished that this cartoonist had been born a few years earlier, or perhaps had been identified more closely with golf in the 'twenties. They were great days. In the wake of Vardon, Braid, Taylor, and particularly Hagen, George Houghton could have snapped up and crystalised hundreds of laughs. Is this nostalgia of mine a sign of old age? I hope not.

Golf keeps you young, and laughing about it keeps you happy. I think this is George Houghton's maxim. He seems to find amusement in everything connected with the game.

Those of you who have read his *Golf Addict Visits the U.S.A.* will need no reminder from me of what goes on at golf on the other side of the Atlantic. I imagine that few of us would find enjoyment in the long hours spent on public golf courses every Sunday morning. But to the author, who indulged freely, every incident, gesture and player was a source of great enjoyment and limitless material.

So far as I am aware George has not travelled into the deep, droll Southern States, and that is an omission which he should remedy. I often visited the immortal Bobby Jones in his southern

CYRIL TOLLEY has played golf for England on no fewer than twenty-seven occasions and it is unlikely that many other golfers can equal this record.

During the nineteen-twenties, with the exception of Bobby Jones, Tolley was the one amateur who stood a good chance of beating any professional anywhere. His particular skill—and the one which never failed to delight the crowds—was an ability to hit the ball tremendous distances from the tee. Twice in one day he drove the eighteenth green on the Old Course at St Andrews; at Troon and elsewhere, he won long-driving competitions against all comers.

Cyril Tolley, who was born in 1895, won the British Amateur Championship at the age of twenty-four; thirty years later he was in the semi-final. In between, he won the British Amateur, for the second time, in 1929, the Welsh Amateur twice, and the French Open Championship twice. In 1948 he was elected Captain of the Royal and Ancient Golf Club of St Andrews.

fortress when he was at the height of his power. Golf addicts who have not been fortunate enough to play golf in Georgia are neglecting an important aspect of their education. Nearly everything that happens there could make a cartoon! Many of Bob Jones's trophies had been lost in a fire which destroyed one of the palatial country clubs. My visit coincided with a celebration to open a magnificent new clubhouse which would house the replaced trophies. Everyone was happy, especially as this time the club was said to be quite fireproof. But in a short while the trophies were again consumed in what was reported as the 'best fire ever'! Everyone thought it a great joke.

I once played with Bobby at Druid Hills Country Club. Apparently I was hitting a few good 'uns, for my long driving was reported in the local press by the late O. B. Keeler, affectionately known throughout the golf world as 'O.B.'. Caddies and chauffeurs in the south are invariably coloured and the morning after the article appeared a non-golfing chauffeur approached me in the car park, saying: 'Massa Tolley, you sure know how to hit a golf ball. Have you ever done two holes in one shot?' Now, the strange thing about this story is that soon after, in South Africa, playing on a course that had seen no rain for four years, my drive to a hole of some 380 yards passed over the green and on to the next green 180 yards further on and nearly holed out!

Of the cartoons in this book, in addition to the odd snatches of conversation, I have a partiality for the incidents which are quite improbable. For instance, I like the one with the elephant. The golf club is swung convincingly while held by the animal's trunk. Also, the left knee is beautifully and correctly bent—to get a full pivot!

The elephant reminds me of Africa, where George Houghton threatens to go one day to expose the addicts of that continent. With due respect to golfers in the Union, and at the same time complimenting them for persevering under conditions made extremely difficult by climate, I must say that I think Houghton will find lots of fun material. On one course during my stay in South Africa we found the terrain very different from anything previously experienced. The local rules provided for the proximity of snakes, removing thorns from the ball when it is on the green, and so on. At Kimberley I once took four putts—my ball having jumped alarmingly in all directions—before the 'thorn rule' was explained.

At Bloemfontein, where no rain had fallen for years, there was no necessity for a 'please replace divots' rule. Further south, notices said: 'Do not kill the tarantulas; they help to keep down the mice and moles . . . ' There is a great untapped vein of golf humour awaiting George in the sunny continent.

At the club for writers of good Forewords I am sure there is a notice saying: 'Don't ramble on'. So let's leave it at that, merely adding 'Thank you, G. H.'

*Cyril Tolley*

# *Is Golf Funny?*

NO. But golfers are. Also, amusing things often happen while the game is played. On those occasions, if you have any sense of humour, your concentration is knocked for six, and then some dullard who hasn't learnt how to laugh wins, and bang goes half-a-crown.

The funniest things in golf are true. The frontispiece incident happened when four professionals were playing an exhibition game on the Blue course at Berkshire. I find this moment very funny and laugh at the memory every time I go to Berkshire. Yet when the incident actually happened we were not amused and those on the tee assumed the correct 'put that woman out' expression. In the bar afterwards someone mentioned what she had said and we roared.

At Pine Valley, that challenging course in the United States, one of our opponents in a four-ball found his ball lodged in a clump of honeysuckle. There is no such thing as an unplayable lie at Pine Valley. You must have a go. My partner and I stood by, trying not to smirk. The unfortunate player examined his ball, turned to partner John Arthur Brown (who happens to be President of the Club) and muttered: 'We don't have problems like this at the office'. Excepting for a tut-tut from John there was dead silence.

When a man laughs aloud on a golf course it is bad. Golf is no joke. The chap who fluffs a shot and then guffaws is depraved. This is not the stuff from which real addicts are made. Laughter comes later—sometimes not until days have passed.

A friend of mine played a round at Letchworth with his wife one summer Saturday evening. They were the last couple out and my pal was cracking the

ball long and straight. At the 13th his drive carried the hill and the ball went bounding downwards out of sight. You cannot see the pin from the tee on this hole for it is in the hollow, but my friend's drive was a peach and there was a reasonable chance of the ball finishing on the green, or very close.

To the couple's surprise, when they got to the top of the hill, the ball was not in sight. They went towards the green and searched for about ten minutes, then proceeded to the next tee muttering about yet another golf mystery . . .

That night, my friend slept badly. Suddenly, he shook his wife and shouted : 'Did you look in the hole ?' The poor girl became conscious and, realising that her addicted husband was still fretting about the drive on the 13th, had to admit that she had not looked in the hole. Each had thought the other had checked on the remote possibility of an ace !

My friend came to life, tugged on his trousers, bounded down stairs, and slammed the door. His wife heard the car starting up. Before settling down again she glanced at the clock. It was half-past-five and a pleasant dawn suffused the room in pink light. She closed her eyes peacefully. But not for long.

The front door opened again and the husband called upstairs : 'You'll have to come. *If this is a hole in one, I need a witness*'.

His sleepy lady in a dressing gown, my friend in a coma . . . they arrived at the club. Hurried across country to the 13th.

It would have been nice to record in this way the story of a perfect hole. But I cannot. When the couple reached the green they found the cup was empty. Deeply disconsolate they made for home.

A workman at the entrance to the course threw over a suspicious glance. My friend's face reddened. 'We've been looking for a golf ball', he said.

Some people might say that very few golfing laughs have anything to do with women. Here is an exception. Freddy has a wife who is golf-addicted. I don't know whether her passion had anything to do with it, but one morning they had a terrific row. My friend stamped from the house, slammed the door and started his day at the office with a scowl like thunder. During the forenoon he met a near-neighbour who asked him if he was moving house.

Freddy shook his head and looked surprised. 'I only wondered', said his friend, 'seeing your furniture out in the garden . . . '

'Heavens !' thought Freddy, 'she's gone home to her mother—and taken the furniture !'

The poor man hurried home. What did he find ? Trouble ? Not a bit of it. Odd items of dining-room furniture were certainly in the garden. The big carpet was hanging from the clothes-line, and into it, with great gusto, his golfing wife was driving practice balls !

The nice thing about golf humour is that it can be enjoyed when courses are enshrouded in the tragedy of deep snow or impenetrable fog. I mean when play is impossible. I used to travel in the train with an addict who, behind his newspaper, chuckled quietly to himself nearly every time we passed Potters Bar golf course. I never asked, but it was obvious that a glimpse of the fairways jogged a pleasant memory.

There are so many pleasant memories. I can honestly say that only playing golf gives me as much fun as drawing it. Although it would be a mistake to imagine that the same thing is funny to everyone, nevertheless I hope some golfers will be able to identify themselves with my characters and laugh heartily. Most of the cartoons first appeared in the Golf Addict calendars. They are now published in this form, on the assumption that more permanency than the usual fortnightly tear-off can do no harm.

Thank you, Cyril Tolley, for so graciously introducing the book. Thank you, Reader, in anticipation of a grin or two.

*George Houghton*

"RATHER PLEASANT, SIR — FOR CONTEMPLATION, WHEN YOU ARE PREVENTED FROM PLAYING ..."

" BUT I CAN'T WAIT AT THE CHURCH FOR TWO-AND-A-QUARTER HOURS ! "

"—AND THAT FOUL OLD PIPE
OF YOURS DOESN'T HELP!"

"THE MOST AWKWARD HAZARD ON THE COURSE"

"PORT OR BRANDY, SIR?"

"THEY PLAYED FOR THE HARLEQUINS!"

"THERE'S NO NEED TO EXAGGERATE!"

"NOW, THIS IS THE POSITION I
WANT YOU TO GET— BUT YOU
MUST BE COMPLETELY RELAXED.."

" IT HASN'T QUITE STOPPED, OLD MAN "

'HE MISSES IT'

"SOMETIMES IT FRIGHTENS ME TO SEE HOW LIKE HIS FATHER HE GETS ...."

THE MYSTIC EAST—AND THE STRAIGHT LEFT ARM THEORY

"MUST I BE INTRODUCED BY A MEMBER?"

"DOCTOR SAYS I'M NOT BEING FAIR TO YOU IF I DON'T TAKE EXERCISE . . ."

"LET ME PUT IT THIS WAY, IF YOU WERE A GOLFER I'D SAY YOU WERE DORMY FOUR DOWN"

" I WOULDN'T MIND SO MUCH IF THEY CALLED THE GOOD PLAYERS RABBITS..."

"NO THANKS, OLD MAN, I JOINED THE LEGION TO FORGET THE GAME ..."

"YOU CONCENTRATE ON HOPING BOB FLUFFS HIS DRIVES AND I'LL WORK ON JACK'S PUTTING..."

'FORE!'

" HE'LL DO ANYTHING TO GROOVE HIS SWING "

"HE'S TRYING TO PROVE THAT FROM OXFORD CIRCUS TO EROS IS A PAR FIVE"

"—AND WE DIDN'T COME TO PARIS TO WONDER WHETHER YOU COULD CLEAR THE ARC DE TRIOMPHE WITH AN EIGHT IRON SHOT!"

"HE ALWAYS PRACTICES DURING SIESTA!"

"I WOULD SAY A SIX IRON SHOT..."

"AWKWARD, OLD CHAP, BUT I SUPPOSE IT'S THE SORT OF THING WE MUST EXPECT IN THE AUTUMN ...."

"I STILL THINK BABY WOULD BE HAPPIER IN HIS PRAM..."

" DON'T WORRY, I'LL TAKE IT CLEAN"

" WE'RE NOT DOING BADLY — THERE'S THE CLUBHOUSE! "

'I SHOULD THINK THEY'RE PRETTY GOOD
–THEY'VE BOTH GOT SHOOTING STICKS!'

'BUT COLONEL, SHOULDN'T WE FIND MY BALL FIRST, <u>THEN</u> GET TO KNOW EACH OTHER BETTER?'

"IT'S OUR SUNDAY MORNING FOUR-BALL"

"THIS ISN'T WHAT I CALL HAVING A NICE WALK..."

'—AND WHAT OTHER MAN LETS HIS WIFE COME TO GOLF WITH HIM?'

" HE HAS A THEORY ABOUT INCREASING THE ARC..."

'THE PRO SAYS I MUST RELAX'

"FORBES BAGGED THAT WITH A BRASSIE SHOT!"

"HE INSISTED ON BRINGING THEM,
— JUST IN CASE . . . . "

'LOOK AT IT THIS WAY, SIR — IS FIFTY POUNDS TOO MUCH TO INVEST IN A FUTURE OPEN CHAMPION?'

'AM I RIGHT IN ASSUMING THAT YOU'VE WON HALF-A-CROWN?'

'QUICK! REPEAT THAT BIT ABOUT HOW EASY IT IS TO HIT A STATIONARY BALL, — I'M GETTING DISCOURAGED!'

"– HE PUT HIS DRIVE TO WITHIN A FOOT OF THE PIN!—TO WIN THE MATCH I HAD TO HOLE OUT IN ONE! WELL—"

" DON'T FORGET TO TELL ME WHEN TO KEEP MY DARNED MOUTH SHUT..."

"JUST HOW I LIKE IT —
NO CROWDS ON THE FIRST TEE..."

"HE'LL NEVER CURE THAT **SLICE** UNTIL HE CHANGES HIS GRIP..."

"KEEP YOUR HEAD DOWN"

"HE'S A 'LIFE-AND-SOUL-OF-THE-PARTY' TYPE
—NEVER MAKE A GOFFER..."

"IT'S HIS FAVOURITE SHOT!"

"WILL HE BE LIVID IF I OFFER HIM A TIP?"

" TEAR UP MY SCORECARD, OLD MAN—I PREFER TO SUFFER IN PRIVATE ! "

" MY HUSBAND SAYS HE <u>HAS</u> TO PLAY GOLF — IT'S THE ONLY WAY HE CAN EXPRESS HIMSELF..."

"MY IDEA IS TO ASK THE MEMBERS TO RALLY ROUND AND LEVEL OFF THAT HILL"

"NOW, WE MUST TRY TO RELAX ..."

"IT'S THE ONLY WAY I CAN GET HIM TO DO THE WEEDING"...

"THEN, BELIEVE IT OR NOT, I MISSED MY PUTT!"

"IN A WAY, I ALMOST PREFER THIS WEATHER"

"I TOLD HIM NOT TO FEED THEM!"

' COME ON CHAPS, IT'S CLEARING '

"PAH! NEW-FANGLED IDEAS! —
I PREFER THE OLD WAY"

" ALLOWING ME BOGEYS ON THE FOUR HOLES WHERE I THREE-PUTTED AND FORGETTING ALL THAT NONSENSE AT THE THIRD AND EIGHTH ... I'VE REALLY HAD AN **EXCELLENT ROUND !** "

"IT'S HIS BEST SHOT"

" DON'T FORGET YOU HAVE A STROKE AT THIS HOLE..."

"THE FUNNIEST THING! – I'VE ARRANGED TO PLAY SINGLES WITH BOTH OF YOU!"

" LET'S FACE IT, OLD CHAP, GOLF JUST ISN'T YOU"

"WHEN MY WIFE ANSWERS THE 'PHONE AFTER LUNCH JUST SAY THAT I'M WANTED AT THE CLUB FOR A VITALLY IMPORTANT ER-MEETING ... I'LL TELL HER ABOUT THE FOURBALL AFTER..."

"I FOUR-PUTTED AND HE SAID BAD LUCK!"

"UGH — IT'S GOING TO BE ONE OF THOSE DAYS!"

"WHAT A LIFE! — FIRST MY WIFE LEAVES ME — NOW THIS SLICE!"

"DON'T FORGET THERE'S A PENALTY FOR GROUNDING YOUR CLUB IN A BUNKER!"

"REMIND ME TO DISCUSS THAT
ONE BACK IN THE BAR....!"

"GO ON, ASK ME WHAT I THINK OF WOMEN GOLFERS!"

"DON'T LET IT PUT YOU OFF, BUT MILLIONS OF TELEVIEWERS ARE WATCHING THAT PUTT!"

"WHEN IS THE COMMITTEE GOING TO DO SOMETHING ABOUT THESE WRETCHED BIRDS?"

'—BUT SUPPOSING ONE HAS SWALLOWED IT?'

'I KNOW IT'S SPRING, DEAR, BUT DASH IT THERE'S A PLACE FOR EVERYTHING!'

"THIS IS WHERE HE MISSES IT AND BLAMES ME"

'I TOLD YOU NOT TO BRING REPAINTS!'

" WEDGE "

"I SUPPOSE IT'S NO USE EXPECTING YOU CHAPS TO KEEP YOUR MOUTHS SHUT"

"I STILL THINK YOU SHOULD BE ABLE TO FIND YOUR BALL WITHOUT ALL THIS FUSS ....."

" THE TIMES I'VE TOLD FRED NOT TO FINISH A SHOT ON HIS BACK FOOT ! "

"HE SAID I COULDN'T REACH THIS GREEN WITH MY DRIVE!"

"... SO, ON THE FIFTH, HAVING A GOOD LIE, I TOOK MY BRASSIE..."

" IF YOU WANT TO TELL ME ABOUT THE BIRDIE YOU'RE GOING TO GET, SPEAK IN A WHISPER— THERE'S A BEASTLY ECHO ! "

"HE LOVES A BALL"

" NOW, CADDIE , DO I HAVE A GO?
— HOPING THAT OUR OPPONENT
WILL FLUFF HIS NEXT, REMEMBERING
THAT I'LL PROBABLY BREAK A CLUB..."

-THE OUTSIDER-

"I DOUBT IF WE'LL GET ANOTHER HOLE FROM THIS BATTERY, SIR"

"I THINK I'D BETTER STAY AT HOME TO-DAY, SIR...AS YOU CAN HEAR, I'VE ALMOST LOST MY VOICE"

"—BUT YOU JUST TRY AND GET HIM TO PADDLE WITH THE CHILDREN...!"

" PSST! — KNOW THE FUTURE, SIR?
—HOW MANY YOU'LL TAKE AT THE SIXTH?"

"I FANCY WE'VE GOT A REAL PROBLEM HERE, SIR"

"WATCH DADDY JUMP WHEN I REMIND HIM HE SHOULD HAVE BEEN ON THE TEE HALF-AN-HOUR AGO.."

" YOU SEEM TO THINK
I LIKE BEING A GOLF ADDICT!"